The Civilization Library
Published in the United States by
Gloucester Press in 1978

Originated and designed by
David Cook and Associates
and produced by
The Archon Press Ltd
28 Percy Street
London W1P 9FF

First published in
Great Britain 1977 by
Hamish Hamilton
Children's Books Ltd
90 Great Russell Street
London WC1B 3PT

Printed in Italy
by Alfieri & Lacroix

Library of Congress Cataloging in Publication Data
Boase, Wendy.
  Early China.

  (The Civilization library)
  Includes index.
  SUMMARY: Discusses early Chinese civilization
including the life, customs, arts, and beliefs of the
people.
  1. China—Civilization—Juvenile literature. [1.
China—Civilization] I. McBride, Angus. II. Dal-
ley, Terence. III. Title. IV. Series.
DS723.B6   1978   951   77–12606
ISBN 0–531–01426–6

THE CIVILIZATION LIBRARY

EARLY CHINA

Wendy Boase

The author wishes to acknowledge
the assistance received from
Arthur Cotterell,
Head of the Department of Adult Education,
North Herts College,
during the preparation of this book.

Illustrated by

Angus McBride and Terry Dalley

Gloucester Press · New York · 1978

39627

The Middle Kingdom

Yin and Yang

The Chinese believed that harmony in the universe depended on a balance between the forces of *Yin* and *Yang*. *Yin* represented everything negative, female, dark, and of the earth. *Yang* stood for the opposites—positive, male, bright, and of heaven. The two forces were shown as a circle divided into two equal parts by a curved line. The design expresses the idea that *Yin* and *Yang* exist in a delicate balance—not in conflict with each other. Evils—droughts, floods or war— were caused by lack of balance between the two. All people tried to live according to the theory of *Yin* and *Yang*.

Traditionally, the Chinese have thought of their country as the center of the world and of civilization. They called it the "Middle Kingdom." The country is divided by three great river systems: the West River in the south, the Yangtze in the middle, and the Yellow in the north. Over these three areas, the climate ranges from almost tropical to almost arctic, and there are high mountains, deep valleys, and wide river basins. Yet this huge, varied country produced a civilization that flourished for over 3,000 years; and, while it has been invaded at times, it has remained a separate and mysterious land.

The first Chinese people settled along the Yellow River in the "Land Within the Passes"—a wedge of country covered with a thick layer of rich yellow earth called loess. The early settlers faced problems of a changeable climate—long droughts, frost and snow, and, worst of all, floods. To survive, they had to find a way to live and work in harmony with nature—a harmony expressed in the ancient theory of *Yin* and *Yang*. The development of water control shows how this theory was used. The peasants worked for the state without pay for one month of every year. They cooperated with nature by digging deeper channels for the water to flow through and irrigate the land which grew food for the 50 million people of the Middle Kingdom.

Yu the Great
According to legend, Yü, "the Great Engineer," was the first to control China's rivers. He deepened the channels so they would not flood and would irrigate the land. The legend says he worked for 13 years without going into his house to rest.

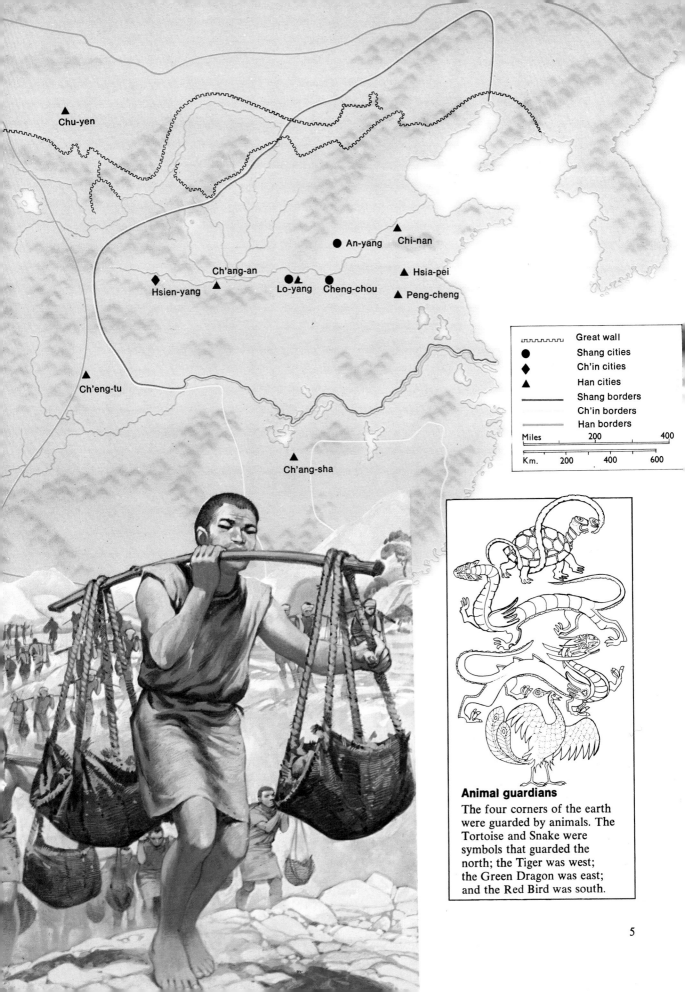

Chu-yen ▲

● An-yang   ▲ Chi-nan

Ch'ang-an
◆   ▲   ●▲   ▲ Hsia-pei
Hsien-yang   Lo-yang Cheng-chou
                                 ▲ Peng-cheng

▲
Ch'eng-tu

▲
Ch'ang-sha

⌐⌐⌐⌐⌐	Great wall
●	Shang cities
◆	Ch'in cities
▲	Han cities
——	Shang borders
——	Ch'in borders
——	Han borders

Miles   200   400

Km.   200   400   600

Animal guardians

The four corners of the earth
were guarded by animals. The
Tortoise and Snake were
symbols that guarded the
north; the Tiger was west;
the Green Dragon was east;
and the Red Bird was south.

The creation of the universe

In Chinese legend, the universe began as an egg. One day the egg cracked open and a man called P'an-ku was born. For centuries he grew taller and taller— while half the eggshell formed the sky above him, and the other half formed the earth below. After 18,000 years, he died, and from his body came the elements of nature. His head formed the sun and moon, his breath the wind, his sweat the rain, and his voice the thunder. Rivers and seas came from his blood, and mountains from his limbs. The fleas on his body became the ancestors of humanity. This myth shows the Chinese view of our humble position in the natural world.

The plan of the universe

Designs on bronze mirrors from the Chou and Han periods showed the Chinese idea of the order of the world. The earth is a square around the central knob. The "T" shapes on each side are sacred mountains that hold up the heavens. The surrounding circles are the outer edges of the universe. Harmony in the universe depended on a perfect balance between *Yin* and *Yang,* the negative and positive forces that act on all things. The *Yin-Yang* theory had a great influence on Chinese life and thought.

The origins of China

Half a million years ago primitive ancestors of modern men and women lived in China. Called "Peking man," they could chip out stone tools, make fire, and speak simple words. In 1500 B.C. their descendants lived under the Shang dynasty. This is the earliest Chinese dynasty, or family of kings, that we know about. Chinese legends tell of mythological rulers in the time between Peking man and the Shang. First, P'an-ku, the creator, then Fu Hsi, the first king. Next, Shen Nung, patron of agriculture and medicine, and Huang Ti, "the Yellow Emperor," under whom art and science flourished. The mythical age ends with Yü the Great Engineer, supposed to be the first ruler of the Hsia dynasty.

No traces of the Hsia have been found. But in the Yellow River valley, the Shang left so much evidence—writings and bronze containers—that the area is called the cradle of Chinese civilization. The Shang were conquered by the Chou. Finally in 221 B.C., in the Ch'in dynasty, China became an empire, with one authority ruling the whole country. Over the next 2,000 years, twenty-five dynasties ruled. The Han dynasty was one of the most successful, and its time is looked back on as a golden age.

The "Yellow Emperor"
Huang Ti is thought of as the founder of Chinese culture, and the ancestor of all emperors.

The "Divine Cultivator"
The first farmer, Shen Nung, is said to have ruled for 140 years.

Time Chart
The outer circle shows the course of Chinese history. The inner circle shows periods of unrest or foreign occupation.

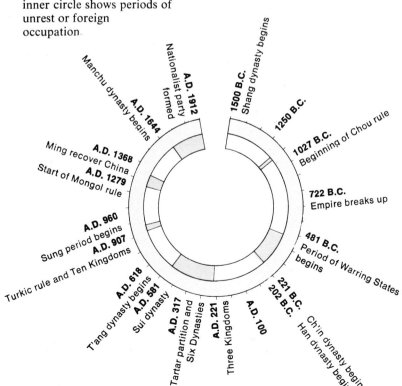

1500 B.C. Shang dynasty begins
1250 B.C.
1027 B.C. Beginning of Chou rule
722 B.C. Empire breaks up
481 B.C. Period of Warring States begins
221 B.C. Ch'in dynasty begins
202 B.C. Han dynasty begins
A.D. 100
A.D. 221 Three Kingdoms
A.D. 317 Tartar partition and Six Dynasties
A.D. 581 Sui dynasty
A.D. 618 T'ang dynasty begins
A.D. 907 Turkic rule and Ten Kingdoms
A.D. 960 Sung period begins
A.D. 1279 Start of Mongol rule
A.D. 1368 Ming recover China
A.D. 1644 Manchu dynasty begins
A.D. 1912 Nationalist party formed

The first Han ruler
In 202 B.C., Liu Pang, a man from a poor family, controlled all the land in the Yellow River valley. He became Emperor Han Kao-tsu.

A turbulent land

The first history of China was written by Ssu-ma Ch'ien, a historian at the time of the Han Dynasty. According to him, the early Chinese dynasties followed a pattern. Each began strong, then grew weaker, declined, and collapsed after several generations.

The first dynasties described by Ssu-ma Ch'ien were the Hsia, the Shang, and the Chou. The Hsia was a legendary dynasty, said to have been founded by Yü the Great. It may actually have existed (about 2000 B.C.) but there is no sure evidence of it. The Shang (1500 B.C.) ruled for about five centuries. They created a great Bronze Age culture. They wove silk, carved jade and ivory, and developed a written language. Their religion, based on ancestor worship, lasted for thousands of years.

But the Shang grew corrupt and superstitious. In 1027 B.C., they were overthrown and the Chou dynasty was founded. The pattern of success, decline, and collapse was repeated. The Chou dynasty ruled for three centuries and then China was thrown into 250 years of unrest. This was called the Warring States period. It ended in the victory of the Ch'in, who created the first great Chinese Empire.

The Ch'in Empire lasted a very short time, but it had

a great effect on Chinese civilization. A strong central government changed the old form of society and regulated everything—laws, language, weights and measures, even farm tools. Bridges, roads, and flood-control programs were begun. The Great Wall was built to keep out the Hsiung-nu —a fierce tribe of nomads. But the emperor, Shih Huang-ti, was so harsh and cruel that rebellion broke out. Liu Pang and the armies of the Han were the victors.

In the Han Empire life improved—paper was invented; astronomers charted the stars; water clocks, water pumps and silk looms were used. The Chinese began to trade silk, gold and cast-iron for pearls, glass, camels and donkeys. They learned new ideas from their neighbors, without giving away many of their own secrets.

China was then the greatest power in all Asia. The Hsiung-nu still threatened, but cavalry and the crossbow (which Europeans learned to use a thousand years later) ensured long periods of peace. The only break in four centuries of Han rule came when Wang Mang, an unpopular rebel, seized the throne in A.D. 9. His short reign divides the Han Empire into two periods: the Former Han (202 B.C.–A.D. 9) and the Later Han (A.D. 25–220).

The Heavenly Horses

Chinese soldiers needed better horses so they could outrun the Hsiung-nu. In Ferghana (Central Asia), a Han ambassador saw the "Heavenly Horses," a spirited breed. Emperor Han Wu-ti tried to buy some from the local king, but failed. He then sent 60,000 men to take some by force. Finally, the local king agreed to trade 3,000 horses for a royal Chinese bride. Each horse was worth 300 pounds in gold.

China in turmoil

In 771 B.C., the Chou rulers were attacked by barbarian tribes and some rebels. After heavy fighting they fled east to Lo-yang. There the dynasty— now called the Eastern Chou— lasted another 500 years. During that time, the Chou states joined together to form a few strong units.

Weapons of war

The Shang army used curved bows, arrows, bronze daggers, axes, and halberds (weapons with a double-edged, pointed blade). Han soldiers carried iron spears and swords, but their deadliest weapon was the crossbow.

The Han court

In the Han dynasty, the emperor's high position above all his subjects was shown by the way he lived. The high wall of the Imperial Palace protected him from common eyes. Servants, officials and special advisers surrounded him. His life was usually bound by formal ceremony. His clothes, his food, the design and decoration of his public halls were all regulated by the seasons of the year, or the ruling forces of nature. But life at the Han court was not always formal, as this scene shows. While the emperor relaxes, government officials, soldiers, and ladies of the court watch a cockfight. A foreign ambassador, perhaps from Asia or Korea, talks with a court official. At the bottom, three Confucian scholars talk among themselves.

The heart of the empire

The people of early China believed their rulers received the Mandate (authority to rule) directly from heaven. The ruler was the highest authority on earth and was called "Son of Heaven." The people owed him obedience and loyalty; and he was responsible for their comfort and prosperity. If he failed in his duties, heaven could give the Mandate to a new hero. This meant that while the throne usually passed from father to son, an emperor's power depended on his own merits, too.

In 221 B.C., the founder of the Ch'in dynasty created the title of Emperor, and called himself Shih Huang-ti, "First Emperor." The dynasty ended when he died, but the system of government lasted over 2,000 years, and the title of "Emperor," was used by every Chinese ruler.

In the Han dynasty, the emperor and the central government had absolute power, but the country was divided into smaller kingdoms and provinces, with governors, kings, and high officials appointed by the emperor. Lesser officials were responsible for religious ceremonies, public building, historical records and taxes. They wore badges on their caps and carried gold, silver or bronze seals to show their rank.

The lesser officials, nobles, knights and scholars formed an upper class of Han society called the *shih*. The next class was the *nung,* or peasants, who produced food for the state. Next were the *kung,* metalworkers and artists. The *shang,* or merchants, and the soldiers were much lower. Han society also included a few slaves.

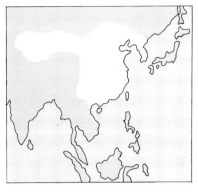

The power of the empire
At the height of the Han Empire, Chinese influence reached across Central Asia.

The Han society
The chart shows the divisions of Han society. People were judged by the contribution they made to the society.

An emperor's palace
A great city, like Ch'ang-an, often had several palaces, built through the centuries by ruling emperors. Each palace usually had one or two halls for public audiences, and a number of towers and gates. A summer palace had fountains and an air-cooling system. Mechanical fans blew air over ice-storage pits and on through ventilators leading to the rooms.

11

The backbone of the country

According to legend, the first Chinese lived like animals—with no shelter or clothing, killing other animals for food. The wise man Yü Tsao taught them to build huts, and the legendary emperor Shen Nung taught them to farm. Since then, agriculture has been the center of Chinese life, and the *nung*—the peasant-farmers—are considered the backbone, or strength, of the society.

But the peasants had a hard life. They lived in one-room homes with earth floors and no furniture. They had to grow food for country and city, for soldiers guarding the borders, and for the landowners who leased them the fields. Floods and droughts were a constant threat, and a large part of their crops (grain in the north and rice in the south) went for government taxes.

In the Han period, some improvements were made: fields were split into furrows and ridges and a new plow was introduced. The use of iron and machinery made farming easier too, but the greatest achievement was the control of water. When the planting and harvesting were finished, the *nung* were put to work (under the ancient system of unpaid labor called corvée) to build dams, waterways, irrigation canals and other public works. In 246 B.C., they built the Kunghsien Canal which, after 2,000 years, is still used. Because the *nung* provided labor on such a large scale, there was no need for a major system of slavery, such as the Greeks and Romans used.

The shaman

The early Chinese believed nature was controlled by spirits. Only the shaman, a kind of medicine man, could make contact with them. The shaman's main task was to bring rain to the fields.

Walled villages

In ancient times, all villages and every group of peasant huts within the villages were surrounded by mud walls. The earth walls of the houses were sometimes covered with plaster.

Plowing

By the 5th century B.C., ox-drawn iron plows were replacing wooden hand-plows.

Reaping

Scythes with cast-iron blades cut grain better than the older stone reaping-knives.

Threshing

Machines increased output. Here a pedal-operated hammer is used to beat the husks off grain.

Labor-saving invention

The Chinese used the wheelbarrow eleven centuries before it was used in Europe.

Terraced slopes

Terraces stop the rich loess soil of the Yellow River basin from being washed down the hill. Loess needs only water to make it very fertile.

Building walls

Dry earth was held in a removable wooden frame and rammed down until it formed a solid wall.

Cutting planks

Chinese workers had a variety of saws. The two-person frame saw worked best.

Ch'ang-an, the capital city

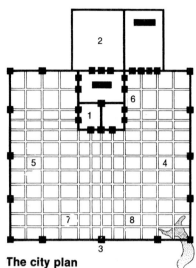

The city plan

From the Imperial Palace (1) and Park (2), the Imperial Way led south to the Meng-ti Gate (3). There were markets to the east (4) and west (5) of it. The important people lived near the palace (6). Most citizens crowded into the small wards (7 and 8).

For centuries, Chinese storytellers have told of the wonders of Han Ch'ang-an: its jeweled palace, the Imperial Park full of rare animals, the ornamental towers and the lakes, the shrines and temples.

The Chinese planned their cities carefully according to the order of the universe and the vital energies of nature. Cities faced south, in the direction of *Yang,* symbol of strength and the positive forces at work in the world. They were square, just as the earth was square in Chinese art. The palace, home of the "Son of Heaven," stood to the north of the city. Streets were divided into walled sections or wards called *li.* The nobles and officials lived near the emperor. The rest of the population lived in the east, except for the *kung* (artisans), who lived and worked in the north and west, and the *shang* (merchants) who at first had to live outside the city walls. Thus the town plan was a symbol of the universe, and of each person's place in it.

The emperor's palace and the temples were very different from the humble homes of most citizens. Palaces were made of mud-brick, but the halls were lined with tiles, and

they were luxuriously furnished. Stone was rarely used. Houses were made of wood or mud-brick. They had court-yards and, often, gardens where trees were planted among stones and water—both important to the Chinese as basic elements of the earth. Each house was surrounded by a wall; every ward was enclosed by another wall; and finally, the city itself was walled. Twelve gates—each wide enough for four carriages to enter—led into the Heavenly City of Ch'ang-an.

The city streets

In the days of the Chinese Empire, there were two great cities: Lo-yang, capital of the Former Han dynasty (202 B.C.–A.D. 9); and Ch'ang-an, capital of the Later Han Empire (A.D. 25–220). There were also large towns spread through the country that were headquarters for the army and local government. In the Han period, between 6 and 10 million people lived in these towns, with as many as 250,000 in Ch'ang-an itself.

The capital was the center of government and of all business. Its streets and marketplaces were crowded with court officials, scholars, soldiers, and workers. The sons of government officials throughout the country came to the capital to be trained for government service at the Imperial University, founded in 124 B.C. Copper and gold coins had begun to replace shells and rolls of silk as money after the Warring States period. For sport, the rich hunted outside the city walls, trapping foxes and deer and shooting geese with arrows.

The great city of Ch'ang-an fell when the Han Empire collapsed. But Ch'ang-an means "Long Security." In the T'ang dynasty, 400 years later, it was restored to glory.

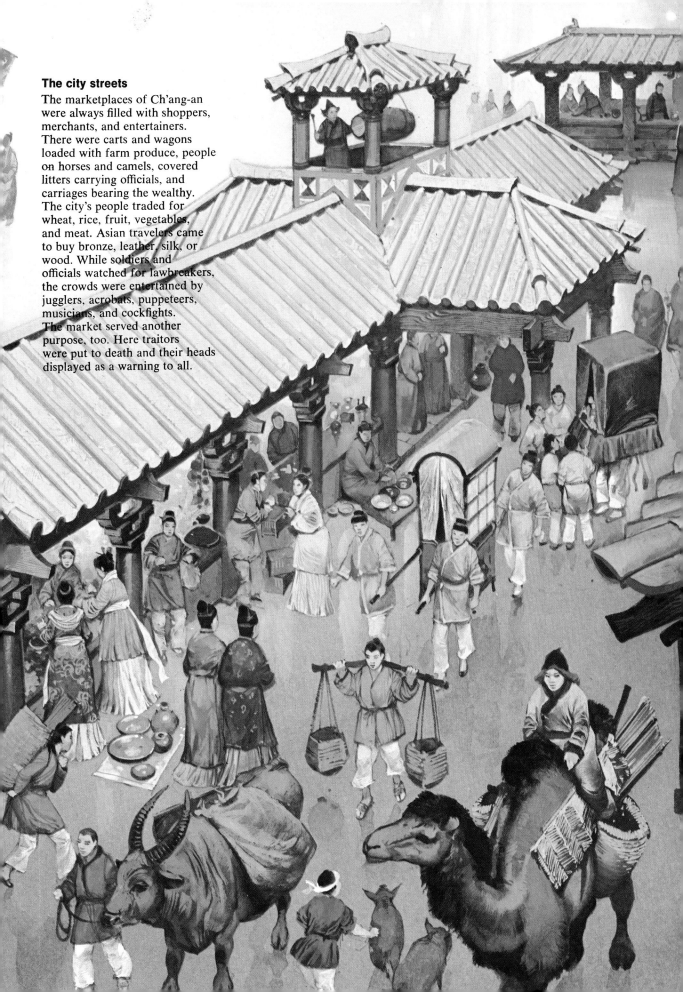

The city streets

The marketplaces of Ch'ang-an were always filled with shoppers, merchants, and entertainers. There were carts and wagons loaded with farm produce, people on horses and camels, covered litters carrying officials, and carriages bearing the wealthy. The city's people traded for wheat, rice, fruit, vegetables, and meat. Asian travelers came to buy bronze, leather, silk, or wood. While soldiers and officials watched for lawbreakers, the crowds were entertained by jugglers, acrobats, puppeteers, musicians, and cockfights. The market served another purpose, too. Here traitors were put to death and their heads displayed as a warning to all.

Science and industry

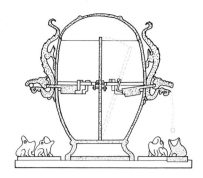

Chang Heng's seismograph
The dragons point in eight directions. If there was an earthquake, a pendulum inside would vibrate and cause a ball to fall from a dragon's mouth into the mouth of a toad below, giving the direction of the tremor.

Producing salt (right)
Salt was mined in western China by 200 B.C. Deep holes were drilled, and brine, or salty water, was drawn up. The water was carried by bamboo pipes to pans and heated. The water evaporated, and salt crystals were left.

The silk industry
Mulberry leaves were grown to feed the silkworm grubs. After they had spun cocoons, the insects were killed. The thread was unwound and then spun into silk.

Early China led the world in science, industry, technology, and invention. Engineering skills developed in response to the need for flood control. The Chinese built an irrigation reservoir about 600 B.C. By the 1st century, they had built the earliest-known arched bridge and iron suspension bridge. In 214 B.C., they completed the Great Wall—the only constructed object visible from the moon.

They mined iron and salt and cast metal weapons and tools 1,700 years before Europeans learned the techniques. Iron and salt were so valuable that the industries were taken over by the emperor in 120 B.C. (Silk production—the oldest, and most profitable industry—was never state-owned, however.)

Gathering mulberries

Feeding the silkworms

Drying cocoons

The Chinese excelled in astronomy and other sciences. They made sundials, water clocks, and a calendar that was still consulted in 1927. By the Han period, they had measured the moon's orbit and charted more than 1,100 stars. They observed sunspots and predicted eclipses. Chang Heng, an astronomer and mathematician, invented a seismograph, an instrument to record earthquakes. Han physicians used acupuncture—a method of healing by piercing the skin at vital points with needles.

Some inventions changed the course of history. Han paper, made from tree bark, hemp, rags, and fishing nets, had a great effect on the spread of literacy when it finally reached Europe in the 9th century. Three Chinese inventions of the Middle Ages—printing, the magnetic compass, and gunpowder—had major effects on the world. Many other inventions—the wheelbarrow, the collar and harness for animals, the long stirrup—also show the superiority of Chinese technology.

Spinning silk from cocoons

Weaving the silk

Drying the silk

The stone of heaven

Jade is highly valued in Chinese tradition, for its beauty and also for its magic. It was believed to stop dead bodies from decaying. A jade *pi*—a disk like the one here—was often buried with the dead. In the Shang period a *pi* symbolized heaven. Jade was rare and difficult to carve because of its hardness. It became a sign of wealth and power.

The arts

Chinese art was first inspired by religion and ritual. About 5000 B.C., Stone Age people placed their dead in pottery urns. Through the following centuries, fine objects—jade rings, carved ax-heads, daggers—were made for burial in tombs. The Ch'in, Han, and later dynasties put pottery figures of servants and bronze horses in the tombs, instead of the live sacrifices the Shang had made. Han tombs were also richly furnished and the walls were covered with carved stones, pottery tiles, or paintings showing happy scenes—dances, musical entertainments, meals, processions.

The ceremonies of ancestor worship produced beautiful objects, too. To honor their dead rulers, the Shang made magnificent bronze objects, decorated with mythical beasts and formal patterns. The early history of bronze is a mystery. There is no evidence of experiments or attempts to make the metal before the sudden appearance of the fine Shang wine and food containers.

Ceramic arts

Fine pottery had been made in China since the Stone Age. At first, the clay was shaped by hand, but by 2000 B.C., the potter's wheel was used for vases and urns, or jars. The clay was fired in kilns and painted with black-and-white patterns. In Han times, colors were used and a mineral called feldspar was put on the clay before it was fired to produce a glazed, shiny surface. In the Sung and Ming dynasties, craftsmen perfected methods of glazing and decorating. Their works were in demand throughout the Far East and the Arab world.

A painted pottery hunter strikes at a cheetah

A glazed pottery tomb guardian

Pottery figure of a woman

Early painted jar

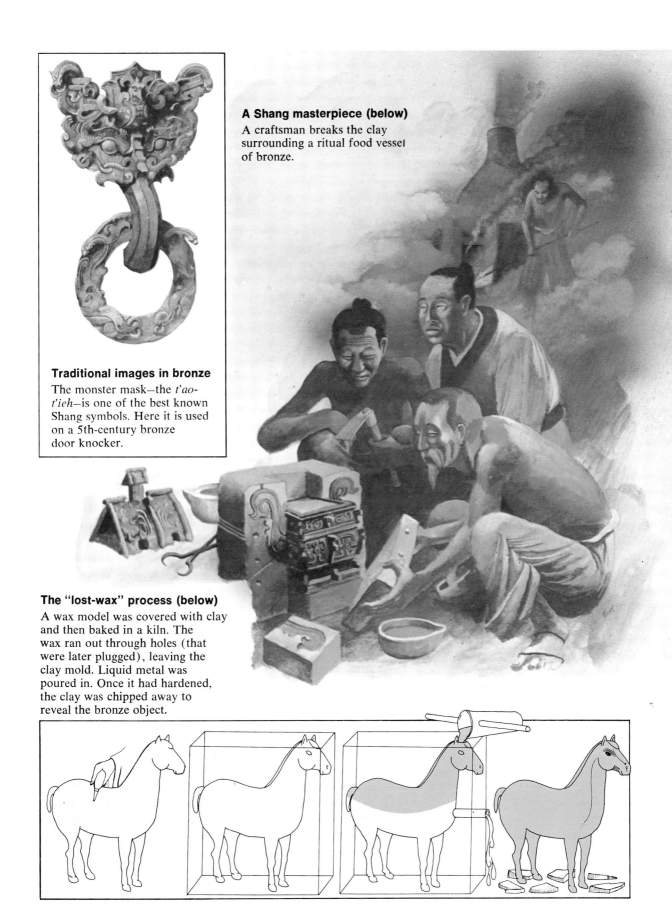

Traditional images in bronze

The monster mask—the *t'ao-t'ieh*—is one of the best known Shang symbols. Here it is used on a 5th-century bronze door knocker.

A Shang masterpiece (below)

A craftsman breaks the clay surrounding a ritual food vessel of bronze.

The "lost-wax" process (below)

A wax model was covered with clay and then baked in a kiln. The wax ran out through holes (that were later plugged), leaving the clay mold. Liquid metal was poured in. Once it had hardened, the clay was chipped away to reveal the bronze object.

The power of the brush

The origin of writing
Fu Hsi, a mythical emperor of China, is said to have invented Chinese writing after studying the marks on a tortoise shell and creating eight basic symbols.

Early script
Oracle bones, used in predicting the future, carry the earliest Chinese writing that has been found. Part of a book of bamboo strips is also shown.

Chinese writing is the oldest script in the world that is still used. Pronunciation has changed over the centuries, but modern writing is still close to the system standardized by the first Ch'in emperor in 213 B.C.

Chinese writing is "ideographic"—symbols or characters are used instead of an alphabet. Each character (ideogram) stands for an object or idea. The Arabic system of numbers is ideographic, too. The symbol *3* stands for an idea. The figure is an ideogram that can be understood by people who read many languages. The meaning of each Chinese character is fixed in the same way. Because of this, the Chinese of today can read the characters written by their ancestors a thousand years ago.

The earliest symbols in Chinese writing were pictographs, or simple drawings, similar to Egyptian hieroglyphs. Each one was a picture of a familiar object—a horse, or mountain. Gradually, the written language was improved; individual parts could have a new meaning—a group of trees meant a forest. The script was extended further by combining pictographs. The sign for wife was made up of the symbols for woman, hand and broom. Over a long period, modern characters were developed, but about 2,000 early pictographs can still be recognized. The sign for tiger still has the distinct tail of the original symbol:

On Shang oracle bones and tortoise shells are the earliest-known writings. Shang kings used them to foretell the future. A priest drilled a hole in the bone and heated it until it cracked. The king's questions about the future were written with a sharp tool on the bone. The answer was interpreted from the pattern of cracks.

In Han times, brushes of deer's hair were used for writing. Government orders and records were kept on wood or bamboo, but scientific works or poetry for the palace library were painted on silk. Paper was invented during the Han period, and was eventually used for books. New forms and styles of literature were created. Some of these were short poems, descriptions of court life, hymns, wedding chants and folk poetry. Ssu-ma Ch'ien wrote the first real history of China about 100 B.C., and the first dictionary appeared in A.D. 121. T'ang scribes copied these ancient writings onto fine paper which they rolled on ivory or wood rods tipped with jade, crystal, or ivory.

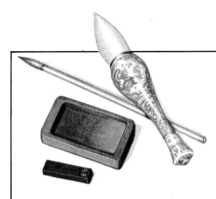

The power of the brush

Calligraphy (beautiful handwriting) did not develop until the sharp writing tools used in the Shang dynasty were replaced by the brush. In Han times, brush painting changed writing from a formal skill into an expressive art. Calligraphers were considered artists, and their tools show the fine nature of their craft. The picture shows two brushes, one of jade, the other of painted porcelain, and an ink cake marked with a delicate design.

Calligraphers studied for many years. They learned to hold the brush upright, and never rest their elbows on the table. There were eight basic strokes to perfect, which were combined in the character for *yung*—"eternity." A legend tells that Wang Hsi-chih, a 4th-century calligrapher, worked for 15 years to master this character.

The ideas and methods of brush writing are like those of painting. Painters and calligraphers used the same inks and brushes to express themselves on silk or paper. Brush parties, like the one below, were pleasant occasions. Scholars drank wine and competed with each other to finish verses of poetry. They were supplied with piles of paper, brushes, and black ink—being mixed by a boy, here.

Painting on silk

Silk production is China's oldest luxury industry. Chinese silk was sold in Roman markets in the Later Han period. Embroidering with silk was an art; and so was painting on silk, as in the picture above.

23

Three ways

Taoism was founded by Lao-tzu, "the Old Philosopher," shown riding a water buffalo.

Buddhism

In the Late Han period, Indians brought the teachings of Buddha, "the Enlightened One," to China. They taught a religion based on meditation and separation from everyday hopes and possessions. Their belief in reincarnation—the soul's rebirth after death in human or animal form—was new to China. By the 6th century, the religion had been accepted along with Taoism and Confucianism.

Unlike the other great empires of the ancient world, China had a number of separate and different religions and allowed them to exist together. The early Chinese worshiped ancestors, as well as gods of nature. Later, the practical teachings of Confucius thrived alongside the mystical religions of Taoism and Buddhism. To the Chinese it was possible to follow all three: Confucianism, Taoism and Buddhism were thought of as "three ways to one goal."

Ancestor worship was the oldest religion in China. Shang kings asked their royal ancestors for advice, and from the Han period on, all Chinese worshiped their ancestors. Early Chinese also believed in the spirits of nature. Through a shaman—a special priest or priestess who spoke to the spirits in a trance—the people prayed to the god of the Yellow River, the earth god, or the spirits of mountains and lakes.

These early religions continued, but times of great trouble led to interest in new ideas. In the Warring States period, before the first Empire, many scholars traveled from state to state explaining their ideas about the right way to live. Two great thinkers, Confucius and Lao-tzu, were among the many who taught at this period. Their teachings were the only ones that survived.

Confucius (551–479 B.C.) taught a practical way of life that is more a philosophy, or way of thinking, than a religion. He taught that loyalty, sincerity, courtesy, and respect for parents were the proper way of conduct. He believed official positions should be earned by talent and education, not by birth. In the Han dynasty, this belief led to a system of state examinations for government workers. The teachings of Confucius influenced Chinese education, government, and social life for 2,000 years.

The Taoists followed a less active way of life and felt that living in harmony with nature was most important. They believed in *Tao,* or the natural "way" to truth, instead of a government of laws and authority. Some Taoists spent their lives studying the wisdom and peace of nature, hoping to become immortal.

Buddhism had few followers in China before the T'ang Dynasty. Then the emperors began to support the new religion. Taoism and Buddhism were mystical religions, with elements of magic and superstition, and although the three religions existed together comfortably, Chinese government and education continued to follow the teachings of Confucius.

Legalism

In the Warring States period, one idea was called Legalism. The Legalists taught that noble behavior would never improve government or society. They advised strict laws and harsh punishments instead. The first Ch'in emperor, Shih Huang-ti, supported their ideas. He ordered other teachings banned and writings burned. Fortunately, Legalism died with the short-lived Ch'in dynasty. In Han times, scholars rewrote the burned books.

Confucius, shown here, taught a philosophy based on good conduct.

Family life

The family was very important in China, in all levels of society, from the peasants to the emperor. Children were taught to honor their parents, and obedience was related to ancestor worship. Some Han emperors set up shrines to their ancestors and appointed priests to look after them. It was believed that when people died, their spirits could influence the lives of their descendants on earth. The family hoped to gain the goodwill of their ancestors by offering food and wine, and praying to their spirits at special home altars. The goodwill could bring many blessings: houses and carriages for the upper classes; for the peasants, enough food and clothing.

Rich families had fine furniture and carpets. They feasted on snails, dogmeat and tangerines, and drank wine, coconut milk and fermented palm juice from silver or gold goblets. They wore silk tunics and jackets, embroidered slippers and gold hair-ornaments.

The poor lived on cakes of millet (a grain), rice, beans, turnips, and fish. They wore straw sandals and clothes woven from hemp.

Ancestor worship
The Shang worshiped only their dead kings, but by Han times, every family made offerings to their own ancestors at home altars.

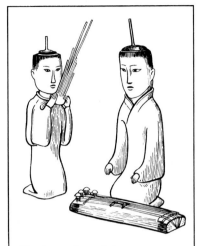

Music and musicians

These wooden figures came from a tomb a little later than the Han period. One holds a panpipe, and the other has a three-stringed zither. Musicians like these played in groups of four or five. Rich people owned their own musicians.

Leisure time

Chinese children played jacks and a game like badminton. Wealthy adults played board games similar to modern backgammon and lotto. Here is a Han-period game called *liu po*. Players throw sticks and move pieces around the board.

Seasonal celebrations

Festivals were for the rich and poor. They included sports, music, dancing, and kite flying, a Chinese invention of the 3rd century B.C.

Cheating death

The jade prince

The Han emperor Liu Sheng was buried in a suit made of 2,498 pieces of jade, a magical stone to the Chinese. It probably took ten years to make.

Early Chinese homes were built of wood and mud-brick, so none have survived. But the tombs of the dead, carved from solid rock or built of stone, have lasted for centuries.

Shang-dynasty tombs have revealed bronze vessels and limestone figures, but the burial chambers themselves were often robbed. Shang ritual funerals were only for their kings. Jade, bronze weapons, ivory, pottery, and musical instruments were buried along with human and animal sacrifices. Sometimes hundreds of people were killed, and once a whole zoo of animals was slaughtered.

Most of these gifts for the dead were buried in the main part of the tomb. This was a deep pit, dug 30 to 40 feet into the ground. The entrances were sometimes guarded by dead sentries armed with bronze weapons. After the burial, the pit was filled with earth.

The practice of human sacrifice ended with the Shang dynasty. From the Han period on, clay figures replaced people and animals. Important officials and the wealthy now built large tombs made of stone, or cut into cliffs. Family respect for ancestors led to a concern for their graves. There were no public cemeteries—the poorest buried their dead on free land near the river or outside city walls.

Royal tombs were the most impressive. Prince Liu Sheng and his wife, Princess Tou Wan, of the 2d century B.C., had rock-cut tombs that could each hold 1,000 people. They were filled with treasures; most amazing were the suits of the royal couple. They were made of pieces of jade sewn together with gold wire. The jade, symbol of heaven, was believed to protect bodies from decay—but it failed to preserve them and only dust remains.

"Let the past serve the present"

The Great Wall

China is a vast country, but it is well protected from the outside world by mountains in the west, jungles in the south, and the sea in the east. Only the open lands of the north have been exposed to the raids of barbarian tribes. To stop these invasions, Shih Huang-ti, first emperor of the Ch'in dynasty, ordered thousands of *nung* to labor for years, to connect three earlier walls into the defense system we call the Great Wall. It ran for 2,400 miles. The wall kept out all invaders from the north— except for the Mongols and the Manchu.

Chinese civilization has flourished for over 3,500 years. Although the ancient imperial system ended in 1912 when the Manchu dynasty was overthrown, the People's Republic of China has maintained many of the great traditions. The Communist Revolution itself fits into the old Chinese pattern of rebellion against weak or harsh rulers. Mao Tse-tung, as leader of the Republic, began an active investigation of history through archaeology with the words, "Let the past serve the present."

In June 1968, soldiers uncovered the treasure-filled tombs of Prince Liu Sheng, who died in 113 B.C., and his wife. News of this unusual discovery spread to the rest of the world. Soon afterward, most of the treasure was exhibited outside China.

Many other sites have been uncovered, and there have been many excavations since the People's Republic was established in 1949. Perhaps Chinese archaeology will continue to bring east and west closer in spite of the invisible barrier which, in modern times, has replaced the ancient one of the Great Wall.

Index

39627